A New True Book

BIRDS WE KNOW

By Margaret Friskey

*This "true book" was prepared
under the direction of
Illa Podendorf,
formerly with the Laboratory School,
University of Chicago*

CHILDRENS PRESS ™

CHICAGO

Turkey

PHOTO CREDITS

James P. Rowan—2, 4, 8, 10, 20 (bottom), 23 (bottom), 24 (2 photos), 25, 33 (left), 36, 38

Reinhard Brucker—14

Jerry Hennen—Cover, 11, 27 (2 photos), 29 (top left), 31 (bottom), 33 (right), 35

Lynn M. Stone—7 (2 photos), 12, 14 (bottom), 16 (2 photos), 19 (2 photos), 20 (top), 21, 23 (top), 29 (top right, bottom), 31 (top), 34, 39, 41, 44 (left)

U.S. Department of the Interior (Dean E. Biggins)—44 (bottom)

Tony Freeman—43

Cover—Red-Tailed Hawk nest with young

Library of Congress Cataloging-in-Publication Data

Friskey, Margaret, 1901-
  Birds we know.

  (A New true book)
  Previous ed. published in 1959 as: My easy to read true book of birds we know.
  For grades 1-3.
  Summary: An elementary introduction to different kinds of birds and some of their more interesting behavior.
  1. Birds—Juvenile literature. [1. Birds]
I. Title.
QL676.2.F74   1981   598   81-7745
ISBN 0-516-01609-1   AACR2

TABLE OF CONTENTS

Most Birds Can Fly. . . 5

Perching Birds. . . 6

Climbing Birds. . . 11

Scratching Birds. . . 15

Night-flying Birds. . . 17

Running Birds. . . 18

Wading Birds. . . 21

Diving Birds. . . 22

Swimming Birds. . . 25

Bird Nests. . . 26

Some Strange Birds. . . 37

Nobody Knows Everything
About Birds. . . 42

Words You Should Know. . . 46

Index. . . 48

Canada geese migrating

MOST BIRDS CAN FLY

All birds have feathers.
All birds have wings.
Most birds can fly. Most
of them are at home in
the air.

PERCHING BIRDS

Birds are alike in many ways.

But birds have different ways of doing things. Each kind of bird has the tools it needs for the way it lives.

Most of the birds we see are "perching" birds. They can lock their toes around a tree branch.

Clark's Nutcracker

Western Meadowlark

Perching birds have four toes. The one in back is about as long as the middle one in front.

English Sparrow

Sparrows are perching
birds. They have strong
bills for cracking seeds.

Many birds eat seeds.
Birds that can get the kind
of seeds they need in
winter do not need to fly
away when snow comes.

Some perching birds eat
insects, bugs, and worms.

Birds that eat insects
must fly away when snow
comes.

Blue Jay

This bird screams its
own name. Jay! Jay! Jay!
A blue jay eats seeds.
A cardinal eats weed
seeds and nuts and grain.

Nuthatch

CLIMBING BIRDS

Climbing birds have feet that help them climb. They have two toes in the front and two in back. They have stiff tails to push against a tree.

All woodpeckers are climbing birds. They have sharp bills and can dig into tree bark for insects.

Woodpeckers live in a hole in a dead tree branch or post.

Listen for the rat-a-tat-tat of a woodpecker at work.

Red-Headed Woodpecker

Grouse

Prairie Chicken

SCRATCHING BIRDS

Some birds are at home on the ground. They have three strong toes for digging, and one small toe high in back.

Great Horned Owl

Barred Owl

NIGHT-FLYING BIRDS

Some birds have wonderful eyes. They can see to fly at night.

An owl can see to fly at night. He flies without a sound as he looks for food, such as mice and frogs.

RUNNING BIRDS

There are birds that run along the water's edge to look for food. Their legs are long.

Sandpipers

Willet

Snowy Egret

Louisiana Heron

Sandhill Crane

WADING BIRDS

Some wading birds look for fish or tadpoles. Their legs are very long.

DIVING BIRDS

Some birds fly over the water. When they see a fish, they dive headfirst for it.

The osprey drops feet-first into the water. He catches a fish with his strong claws.

Brown Pelican

Roseate Tern

Mallard Duck

Canada Geese

Herring Gull

SWIMMING BIRDS

Birds that swim have webbed feet. They use their feet as paddles.

BIRD NESTS

In most bird families the father bird and mother bird build a nest together.

The mother bird lays eggs. She sits on them to keep them warm until they hatch.

Great Blue Heron nest

Robin sitting on eggs

Sometimes the father bird brings food to the mother bird. He sings to her.

Sometimes the father bird sits on the nest so the mother bird can fly to find food and use her wings.

Top left:
Red-Tailed Hawk nest,
young are hatching

Top right:
Young Brown Pelican

Bottom:
Young Cardinals

Both mother and father
birds feed the baby birds.
They show them how to fly
and to hunt for food.

Birds build many kinds of nests.

The mother oriole weaves a hanging nest of grass and string.

The whip-poor-will makes only a dent in the leaves on the ground.

Bobolinks build in the tall meadow grass. They use grass and weed stems.

Laughing Gull on nest

Redwing Blackbird nest

The goldfinch builds near the ground. The nest is lined with thistledown.

The crested flycatcher uses old snake skins in its nest. It uses other things, too.

Robins build with sticks and mud. They line the nest with grass.

Cliff Swallows in nests

Robin's nest

Barn swallows use mud,
too. But they line the nest
with feathers.

Some birds will use a little bird house.

A kingfisher builds in a hole in a mud bank.

A tern sometimes lays its eggs on bare rock. The eggs look like little rocks.

Nest of the Least Tern

A Hummingbird's nest is shaped like a cup.

A hummingbird's nest
is made of soft plant down
and spider webs. It is no
bigger than a marshmallow.

Penguins

SOME STRANGE BIRDS

Penguins are birds. They can swim, but they cannot fly.

Ostrich

An ostrich can run like a racehorse. But it cannot fly.

Some birds do strange things.

The butcher bird hangs his food on a bush.

The lazy cowbird lays its big eggs in other birds' nests.

Cowbird egg in a Redwing's nest

A pelican has a lunch pail in its pouch. It can carry fish there.

White Pelican

NOBODY KNOWS EVERYTHING ABOUT BIRDS

People are trying all the time to learn more about birds. The more they learn, the more wonderful and interesting birds become.

Better airplanes have
been built because of what
people have learned from
birds.

Left:
Barn Owl

Below:
Evening Grosbeak

Birds are important in our world.

They eat many insects that hurt crops.

They help scatter seeds. New plants grow from these seeds.

They brighten woods and fields with color. Birds fill our world with song.

WORDS YOU SHOULD KNOW

alike (ah • LYKE) — the same; similar

bare (BAYR) — without a covering; naked

bark — outer covering of the trunks, branches, and roots of trees

bill — the hard mouthparts of a bird; beak

branch — part of a tree or shrub that grows out from the trunk or limb

bright (BRITE) — strong in color; happy; cheerful

bug — any insect or animal like an insect

bush — a woody plant that is smaller than a tree and has many branches; shrub

claw (KLAW) — sharp, curved nail on the toe of a bird

climb (KLIME) — to go up, over or through; to go higher

crack (KRAK) — to break open; split

crested (KRESS • tid) — a bunch of feathers on a bird's head

crop (KROP) — plants grown for food

dent — a hollow place in a surface; a sunken area

different (DIFF • uh • rent) — not the same; unlike

dive (DYVE) — to go headfirst into water

feather (FEH • ther) — a part of the bird's skin that covers it

field (FEELD) — a large, open area of land

grain (GRAYN) — the seed of wheat, corn, or rice

hatch (HACH) — to come out of the egg

hurt — have a bad effect on; harm

important (im • POR • tent) — having great value

insect (IN • sekt) — a small animal with six legs and three body parts

interesting (IN • ter • ess • ting) — to hold attention

lazy (LAY • zee) — not willing to work

learn (LERN) — to gain knowledge or skill through study

line —to cover the inside of something with a layer of material

lock —to hold tightly in place

marshmallow (MARSH•mell•oh) —soft, white candy

meadow (MEH•doh) —a grassy area

migrating (MY•grayt•ing) —moving from one part of the country to another

mud bank —ground near water that is wet, soft, and sticky

paddle (PAD•il) —a tool used to move through water

perch —to hold onto a branch

plant down —soft, fine material from a plant

pouch (POWCH) —a bag of skin or flesh used to carry things

racehorse (RAYSS•horss) —a horse that runs in a speed contest

scatter (SKAH•ter) —to spread about

scream (SKREEM) —a loud cry or shout

seed —the part of a flowering plant that can grow into a new plant

sharp —not rounded; pointed

stem —main supporting part of a plant; stalk

strange (STRAYNJ) —odd; unusual; different

stiff —not easily bent

tadpole (TAD•pole) —stage of frog or toad development when they have long tails and breathe with gills.

thistledown (THISS•il•down) —soft, fine material from a plant with sharp points

tool —something used to do work

wade —to walk in water

weave (WEEV) —to make something by passing strands over and under other strands

webbed (WEHBD) —having skin that connects the toes

wonderful (WON•der•full) — marvelous; very good

worm (WERM) —an animal with a soft, long, rounded body and no backbone

INDEX

airplanes, 43
baby birds, 29
barn swallows, 33
bills, 8, 12
blue jays, 10
bobolinks, 30
bugs, 9
butcher birds, 39
cardinals, 10
climbing birds, 11, 12
cowbirds, 39
crested flycatchers, 32
diving birds, 22
eggs, 26, 34, 39
father birds, 26-29
feathers, 5
feet, climbing birds, 11
feet, swimming birds, 25
flycatchers, 32
flying, 5
goldfinches, 32
hummingbirds, 35
insects, 9, 12, 45
kingfishers, 34
mother birds, 26-29
nests, 26-35, 39

night-flying birds, 17
orioles, 30
ospreys, 22
ostriches, 38
owls, 17
pelicans, 40
penguins, 37
perching birds, 6-10
robins, 32
running birds, 18
scratching birds, 15
seeds, 8, 9, 10, 45
sparrows, 8
swallows, 33
swimming birds, 25
tails, climbing birds, 11
terns, 34
toes, climbing birds, 11
toes, perching birds, 6, 7
toes, scratching birds, 15
wading birds, 21
webbed feet, 25
whip-poor-wills, 30
wings, 5
woodpeckers, 12
worms, 9

About the Author

Margaret Friskey, Editor Emeritus of Childrens Press, was Editor-in-Chief of the company from its conception in 1945 until her retirement in 1971. It was under her editorial direction that CP expanded to become a major juvenile publishing house. Although she now has more time, her days are by no means quiet. She spends time with her children and grandchildren, all of whom live near enough to her little house in Evanston to visit often. She also has more time to concentrate on her writing.